ON THE MOVE

BOATS

**For a free color catalog describing Gareth Stevens'
list of high-quality books and multimedia programs,
call 1-800-542-2595 (USA) or 1-800-461-9120 (Canada).
Gareth Stevens Publishing's Fax: (414) 225-0377.
See our catalog, too, on the World Wide Web:
http://gsinc.com**

Library of Congress Cataloging-in-Publication Data

Stickland, Paul.
   Boats / Paul Stickland.
     p. cm. — (On the move)
   Includes index.
   Summary: Illustrations and brief text present various types of
boats: ferries, rowboats, sailing ships, oil tankers, and more.
   ISBN 0-8368-2151-3 (lib. bdg.)
   1. Ships—Juvenile literature. 2. Boats and boating—Juvenile
literature. [1. Boats and boating. 2. Ships.] I. Title. II. Series:
Stickland, Paul. On the move.
VM150.S87   1998
623.8—dc21   98-14525

This North American edition first published in 1998 by
Gareth Stevens Publishing
1555 North RiverCenter Drive, Suite 201
Milwaukee, Wisconsin 53212 USA

© 1991 by Paul Stickland. Produced by Mathew Price Ltd.,
The Old Glove Factory, Bristol Road,
Sherborne, Dorset DT9 4HP, England.
Additional end matter © 1998 by Gareth Stevens, Inc.

Gareth Stevens series editor: Dorothy L. Gibbs
Editorial assistant: Diane Laska

Printed in Hong Kong

1 2 3 4 5 6 7 8 9 02 01 00 99 98

ON THE MOVE

BOATS

Paul Stickland

Gareth Stevens Publishing
MILWAUKEE

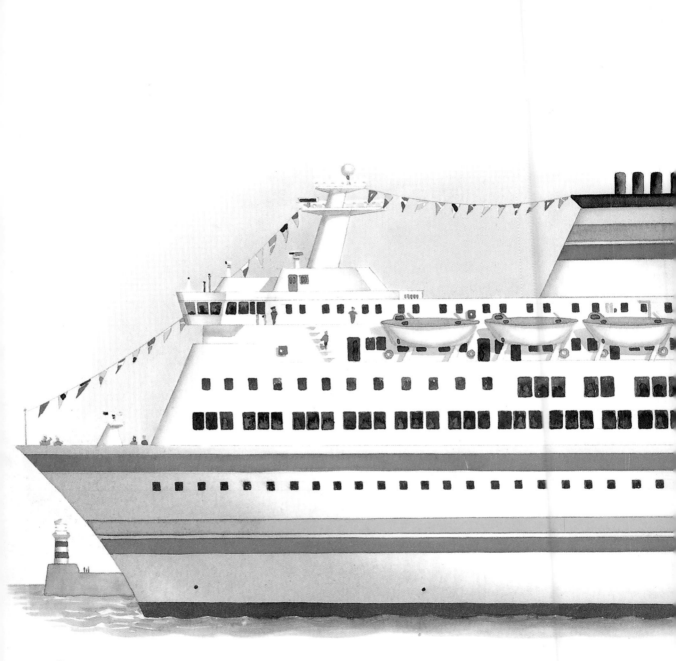

4

A ferryboat takes cars and trucks and passengers across the water.

All boats must be repaired and repainted from time to time.

Oars help pull a rowboat through the water.

Engines make powerboats go very fast.
Some have large, comfortable cabins.

A hydrofoil is a passenger ferry that skims across the water at high speeds.

Old wooden sailing ships had many sails
to catch the power of the wind.

An ocean liner needs a powerful tugboat to help pull it into the harbor.

When an oil tanker is full of oil, it is so
heavy it takes an hour to stop moving.

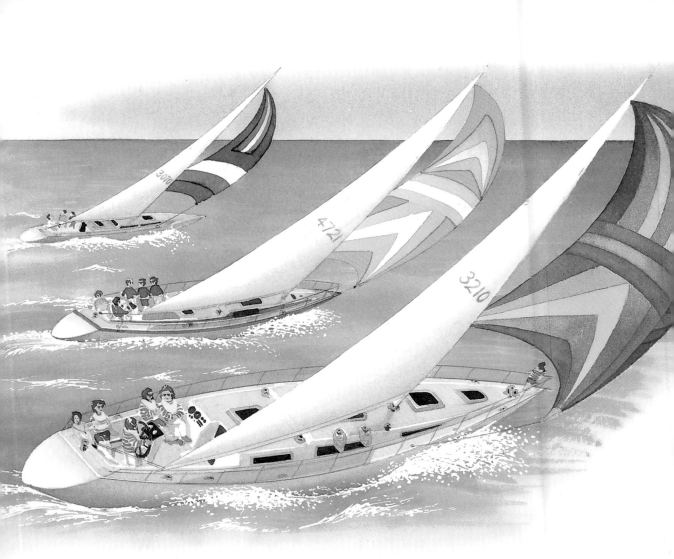

Some yachts are built for speed.

They can race across the sea.

GLOSSARY

cabin — a room or space inside some boats that might have a kitchen, beds, and a bathroom.

harbor — a protected area of water where boats stay when they are not sailing anywhere.

hydrofoil — a very large boat with metal fins that lift it off the water when it is going very fast.

passengers — people who ride in a boat or in some other vehicle, such as a car, bus, train, or airplane.

skim — to move quickly over the very top of something.

yacht — a boat that has sails and a motor and is used for fun, racing, and relaxing.

INDEX